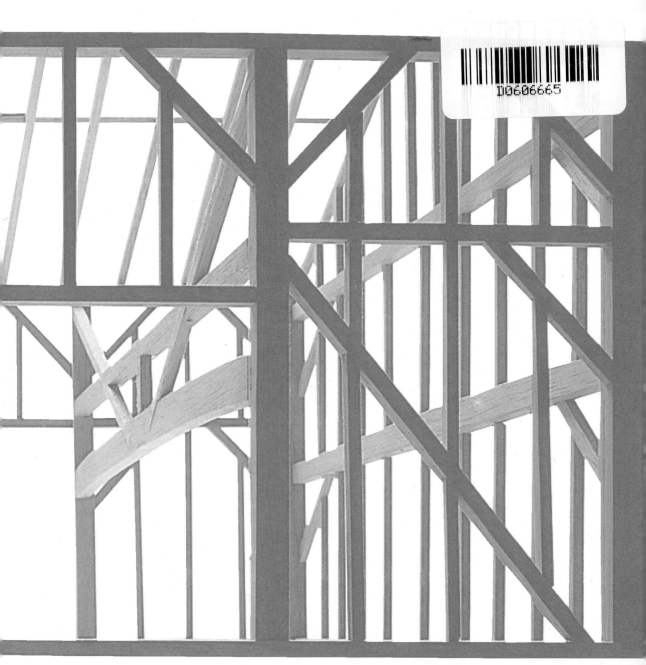

The Essential Book of BARNS
Discovering the Design, Function, and Form

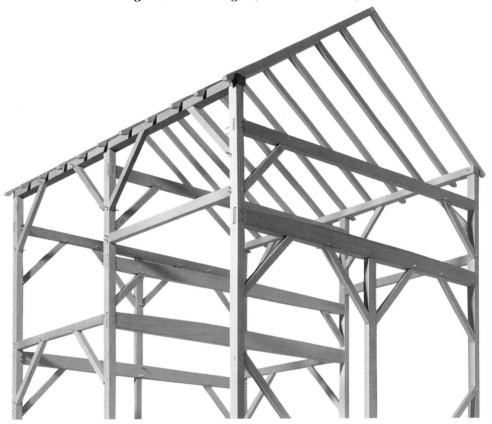

David Larkin

UNIVERSE PUBLISHING

First published in the United States of America in 1995 by
UNIVERSE PUBLISHING
A Division of Rizzoli International Publications, Inc.
300 Park Avenue South
New York, NY 10010

95 96 97 98 99 / 10 9 8 7 6 5 4 3 2 1

Printed in Singapore

Library of Congress Cataloging-in-Publication Number: 95-060820

THE BARN has its place in the history both of Europe and America; it has been celebrated in painting, poetry, and literature throughout the years; it is one of the single most recognizable structures in the world.

For all that it has become, the barn's original purpose was fairly simple: it was a place of storage. Farmers needed space to house their animals and the food that had to last throughout the winter. The barn became the heart of the farm as it protected the farmer's most important resources.A strong barn was often constructed even before a permanent house. There is perhaps no other structure that is as purely functional.

The plan for the first American barn was based on that of medieval European barns, adapted by the settlers to fit their needs in the climate and landscape of the New World. The European barn, with its wide center aisle, high roof, and narrow side aisles set off by supporting columns, was similar to that of the basilican plan of the early Christian churches. The center aisle became the barn's threshing floor while the side aisles became space for storing hay and for animal stalls. It was this basic plan that was adapted by the many different groups who made their way to the colonies. The refinements made to the original plan were determined again by purely functional reasons. The area's climate, the specific purpose of the barn (for later there is specialization among farmers), and the surrounding landscape, along with the resources, tools, and time available, all contributed to the great variety of barns, and the differences even within a specific type. All refinements were made in the name of practicality and function so that the farmer was building a structure meant solely to fit his needs.

It was the Dutch settlers who brought the basilican plan barn to the New World. Found predominantly in New York and New Jersey, these are some of the oldest barns in the nation. Earlier English settlers had introduced a smaller barn with a side entry. Originally appearing in New England in the seventeenth and eighteenth centuries, this type has also been found in many variations throughout Canada and the United States, the form lending itself to enlargement through the addition of lofts, lean-tos, and ells. Constructed of wood, brick, or stone, the English barn is distinguished by the placement of the wagon door at the center of the long wall, and by its size, which was always three bays. In English barns, the threshing floor ran the width of the interior, rather than the length; the central bay, therefore, consisted of both the threshing floor and the wagon entry.

The Pennsylvania bank barn became an archetypal American barn. In Switzerland and Bavaria, where the land is mountainous, farmers adapted by building into the slope of the land. While the landscape of the New World was not as hilly, they utilized the same techniques and innovated the first multilevel barns in the colonies. Built on a stone foundation and built into the side of a hill—hence the name "bank"—this new refinement allowed animals and wagons easy access to the yard and provided livestock and grain separate quarters. This efficient and practical barn remained popular throughout the twentieth century. Some farmers built one or both gable ends out of stone, and there are even instances of the entire barn being built of stone, resulting in a majestic and lasting structure.

Farming became more specialized and the barns were built to accommodate more specific needs. Dairy farming called for interior and exterior adaptations and added new elements to the vocabulary of the barn. The silo was added to store corn, enabling farmers to feed their cows throughout the winter; the cows could then give milk year-round, increasing the farmer's productivity and income. (Silos were originally stone structures built into the ground to make them airtight and protect from spoilage. Farmers discovered, however, that if built out of stone, a silo is equally protective above the ground.) A lower roof was added to the outside of the barn to allow the farmer to work in snow or rain. The haymow increased in size as the threshing floor vanished, and extensions were added to the exterior to protect the haymow from inclement conditions.

The most important element of the barn is its roof, which determines both the interior and exterior character of the barn. The earliest covering material was thatch, later wood, and eventually shingles. The original pitched roof was modified into the gambrel roof, which allowed for the space that more prosperous farmers needed. Ventilating cupolas and weather vanes became two of the distinctive and useful additions to barn roofs. Victorian flourishes are seen on some late-nineteenth-century barns, giving them an elegant presence that belies the practicality of the structure. The early wooden barns were not painted but simply allowed to weather. Hex signs painted on the sides of barns are evident throughout the central United States, particularly in Pennsylvania. Originating in Europe, these symbols were believed to guard against witches and other evil. However, it is now thought that these were purely decorative elements to the nineteenth-century barns.

Over the past several decades, due to changes in the economy, technology, and industry leading to the overall decrease in individual farming as a living, many barns have fallen into disuse and eventually abandonment or destruction. However, perhaps because of our deep connection to them, barn renovation has become popular. Preservation societies across the United States have adapted barns for new uses, helped restore old barns to working condition, and converted them for residential or business use.

The sight of a barn can still inspire awe, not only because of the power of its size and the beauty of its structure, but because of what it stands for as well: human perseverance, ingenuity, and craftsmanship.

The very first barns, which originated in Northern Europe probably
looked very much like this building from the windswept North Sea
coast of Denmark. The roof is covered in sod due to the scarcity
of wood. This was also a common building practice in nineteenth-
century Nebraska and the western prairies, where timber was
scarce and farmers reverted to the Old World methods of
construction and shelter.

In cold climates the house and barn were often separate areas under the same roof. This restored and renovated structure, built in Midlum, Holland originally in the 1700s, is an example of the head, neck, and body plan: the head is a small house containing sleeping and living quarters; the neck consists of a kitchen, milk cellar, and churning room; and the body accommodates the stalls, threshing floor, and barn area.

This thatched hipped-roofed Dutch barn is a well-preserved example of the house-barn combination.

The board across the bottom of this double doorway of a barn in Holland is probably a remnant of the original threshold. Originally built to retain the grains while the wind blew through the open doors as the farmer separated grains from the stalks and the chaff, the "threshold" became a standard element in building a doorway.

A center pole and winding mechanism
for a hay barrack. The roof is raised
and lowered notch by notch to
accommodate the use of the hay crop.

Before the Dutch settled in the Hudson Valley in America, timber resources throughout Europe were severely depleted. The New World barn builders were very grateful for the stands of fine virgin timber. Most of the good, straight trees in Europe were used for building large ocean-going vessels, which often consumed an entire forest. One of the reasons for building ships was to discover countries where timber could be found. In fact, early British settlement of Australia was a result of the search by the British for pine for masts. Discovering the pines of Norfolk Island were useless, they instead set up a penal colony there. This detail of a working barn in northern Holland shows how farmers had to hunt for, patch, and reuse the timber numerous times. The peg holes in the main beam show evidence of many years of use.

Cupolas were originally constructed as a source of light and ventilation. Later they also took on an ornamental purpose, expressing something about the taste and wealth of the farmer. The size of the cupola itself — sometimes as big as ten square feet — and the decorative elements used — latticework, cornices — increased with the success of the farmer. The prominent cupola on the roof of a barn on Martha's Vineyard gives the impression of an even bigger structure.

This barn in Old Bethpage Village, New York, is known as "English" or "Scotch-Irish" in style. Traditionally, these always had a side entry. The Dutch barns in the New World, in contrast, had a gable or end entry.

A view from the threshing floor of a barn in Lancaster County, Pennsylvania, now retired from its original purpose. Barns in this part of the country often had room for a built-in corn crib in the main structure.

It is not just the corn that is growing around this building
that indicates its use. The gaps between the horizontal boards
on either side of the sliding gable doors provide ventilation,
and it is this function that denotes it as a corn crib barn.

The Anatomy of a Barn

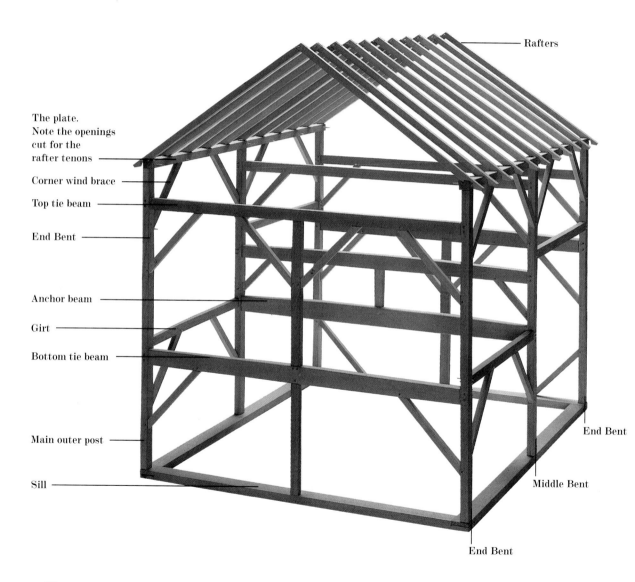

Rafters

The plate.
Note the openings
cut for the
rafter tenons

Corner wind brace

Top tie beam

End Bent

Anchor beam

Girt

Bottom tie beam

Main outer post

Sill

End Bent

Middle Bent

End Bent

Many hands make equal work.
Here the bents of an historic barn in Old Sturbridge Village,
Massachusetts, are raised in the traditional way: by hand.

The barn at Old Sturbridge Village, with
its frame and rafters up after the first day
of raising, shown on the previous page.

Today there are expert timber framers
and barn restorers who can still use
the traditional tools shown here.
The large chisel at right, called a slick,
allows the builder to smooth the
rough surfaces of the wood.

The intensity and pleasure of the labor involved in raising a barn is something few people experience today. The process of working with available natural resources, choosing the plan and the tools, and the integral involvement of manual building contribute to making the barn an important and mythical structure.

This is a fine example of a restored fifteenth-century English aisle barn, which is now used as a community center. The original large beams were blackened by a fire, and the restorers reported that the timber, being so hard and ancient, made it difficult for the flames to take hold. Interestingly, the soot effectively keeps away any insect trouble. The slightly curved diagonal beams are called passing braces and are a legacy from ancient shelters when buildings just had cross members and no walls. Records show that these beams were in fact grown and pruned in groves by monks, specifically for this building. They were relatively young trunks, used for their flexibility, as the use of steaming to bend wood was not known to the monks.

The vast walls of this barn in Lancaster County, Pennsylvania, need the extraordinarily sturdy interior frame for sufficient support. Built in the late 1700s, the timbers are fastened to the wall with iron tiebacks. These tiebacks often had exterior adornments, such as metal plates with stars. The slots in the wall — called loopholes — allow for light and ventilation. The braces, which are extremely long, support the weight of the roof.

Pleasant Hill Shaker Village, Kentucky.
Though as big as a barn, this magnificent
structure is in fact a corn crib built to store
the harvest for an entire Shaker community.

This view into the hayloft of a
working barn in New York State
shows the winter supply of hay.

previous pages
Many historic barns in their original farmsteads, can be visited, such as Howell Farm in Mercer County, New Jersey. At this living history farm, the barn in the center of the picture accommodates the cattle and horses that are used in an interpretive study program.

The forebay, shown here in this well-maintained and restored Pennsylvania bank barn, was originated by the German and Swiss who settled in Pennsylvania. Supported by an arcade, the forebay provided protection from the elements, allowing farmers to work under almost any weather conditions. The advantages of this feature eventually made it a standard element in nineteenth-century Pennsylvania barn design.

This Shaker work building originally served
another purpose in the Harvard, Massachusetts,
Shaker community. Today it is used as a barn,
and is usually filled to the rafters with hay.

As settlers moved westward they brought with them the same architectural traditions that were common in the east. This barn complex looks typical of a rural New Jersey or Pennsylvania dairy barn—note the silo and the gambrel roof—until we see the Cascade Range of Washington State in the distance.

The onslaught of development into rural areas often leaves the overtaken farm structures marooned; soon after, they are bulldozed out of history.

This well-maintained New Jersey bank barn was rescued from such a fate. After being patiently measured and drawn, it was carefully disassembled and then moved and restored in the Beaverkill Valley in New York.

If a barn has been well-built and well-pegged, it is easier to take apart. The model structure, shown in scale to the restored original, was constructed to show the new owners how soundly the structure is built. Note the number of wind braces used to assure its stability.

This small, well-cared for barn in Salem County, New Jersey,
is similiar in structure to the framed example opposite.
The timber frames of barns are rarely exposed on the outside.
It is the layout of the timber frames which articulate and
modify the space inside a barn, and establish its character.

The interiors of barns have much in common with the
characteristics of local churches. In a flat or gently
undulating landscape, the barn is frequently seen in
silhouette, and is, apart from the church, often the
largest building in the parish.

This Pennsylvania bank barn was
converted for family relaxation when
the farmer retired. This is the building
that has the built-in corn crib
shown on page 21.

This barn now rests on the south coast of Martha's
Vineyard. Originally it was part of a farm overtaken
by developers in New Jersey. It is now used as
a summer home connected to a small cottage.
The steps lead up to a sleeping loft.

The barn often had a life that was less
utilitarian. On Saturday nights farm
people would gather for a dance.
This converted barn in Peterborough,
New Hampshire, is ready for a
wedding celebration.

A fine example of conversion to residential use.
This corner of a large Massachussetts barn is now the
kitchen area that fits between the bents in a corner bay.

There are no white painted walls "exposing" the beams.
Instead, the original color of unpainted timber remains
with a tint derived from many years of contact with hay.
The original internal frames and boards had originally
hung forks and barn coats. These timbers now
appropriately accommodate the cook's tools and utensils.

This barn was originally built in Northampton
County, Pennsylvania, but was re-erected in
Southampton, New York, saving it from
demolition due to highway development.
It is now a summer home.

Note the unusual vine branches in the loft
banister. A subtle design element, it
contrasts well with the original surroundings.

Here is an imaginative use of the stable portion of Theodore Roosevelt's Oyster Bay, New York, barn complex. The stalls and the original structure remain intact and serve as a fine conservatory.

With more advanced tools and stronger building materials
in the mid-nineteenth century came the introduction of
the highly efficient sliding door. The convenience of this
innovation led to its use in both interior and exterior
doorways, and for large and small doors.
Pictured here is the sliding door in
Theodore Roosevelt's barn in Oyster Bay, New York.

A hayloft becomes an intimate sleeping area.
Note that no part of the original structure
has been compromised.

In residential barns it is best to keep furnishings subtle,
so as not to compete with the magnificence of the
surroundings. Note the corner gunstock post
and the abundance of wind braces.

Here is a good example of a barn converted in Britain for office use. The original entrance bay now becomes a screened-in porch. The barn siding is finished with creasote stain, which is very common on farm buildings in southern and eastern England. Interestingly, in the horse country of Kentucky, this color and finish is very popular.

Residential barn conversions are extremely popular but are often incorrectly planned and executed, altering the original character of the building and diminishing it visually. A successful barn conversion, however, is often the only way to save a barn from complete loss. In the impressive conversion of a barn in Kent, England, pictured here, the wagon door has been converted into a large window bay allowing for natural light.

This Delaware Valley computer store in a friendly, renovated red barn is much more charming than any store in today's malls.

Conway House Museum, Camden, Maine.
This magnificient shingled barn tells us its
location by its appearance, for it was very
common on the coasts of New England to
weatherboard the coastal buildings with
cedar shingles to prevent damage by water.

The difficulty of using so much space in a
barn converted for residential purposes is
usually the problem of getting aloft.
Here, within the converted structure,
a stairway rises to the level of the original
hayloft, independent of any of the main
structural posts.

This barn, originally from Vermont, is shown in the process of being converted to a home in Long Island, New York. The original now sits on a new storey which was the stone foundation and cowshed at its original location. Therefore, we can see how little of the original structure has been compromised even with twice the amount of volume added to the new home.

This 1820 barn has been converted to
a residence in Beaverkill Valley, New York.
Only the bottom floor is insulated and can
be inhabited year-round.The upper floor
is used only for storage during the winter
and for relaxation and parties in the
warmer months.

This 200-year-old barn in northern Holland no
longer serves its original purpose, yet it is still used
by the farmer as a store and
workshop. Note the original post and beams
which are evidence of when, many years ago,
timber was seriously depleted.

A "new" barn on a Dutch farmstead.
No longer having to make do with dwindling
timber resources, the more recent structure,
with its sawn timbers and added natural light
from low windows, now houses the livestock.
The exterior is shown on page 8.

This barn, now converted to a magnificent home, originally
rested one field away from its new site.

Restored to its original appearance, the interior of this New Jersey barn is extremely impressive. The swing beams span thirty feet and are connected to the top of the flanking posts by long passing braces.

The primitive beams, braces, and rafters of the small
Dutch barn add great charm. This appeal was
unintentional, however; it was the result of the
limited timber supply in Holland at the time.
In fact, the shortage necessitated the floating
of logs from Scandinavia for building.

Those wishing to live in a restored barn might just
consider the original ways in which these buildings
combined living and work. This barn in Holland
shows how close the juxtaposition of animal
and human shelter could be.

The most common color for barns in North America is red. It is common because a large building is expensive to paint and economic farmers traditionally were responsible for originating this color themselves. They would use a combination of linseed oil made from the flax in their fields, casein from the milk of their cows, and red ochre or oxide from the earth itself. This combination of ingredients was traditionally used by Scandinavian farmers. Today this color is still used in Northern Europe. There is still evidence in Southern Germany and Switzerland of dried ox blood supplying the color for barn siding in that region.